infinity minus one

Also by John R Snyder:

Tending the Light: Essays on Montessori Education.
Burton, OH: North American Montessori Teachers
Association, 2015.

infinity
minus one

John R. Snyder

Cover photograph © Nicholas Pippins. Used with permission.

DEDICATION

For Kathy, whose love and companionship
has for the past 38 years delighted me, challenged me,
instructed me, inspired me, and sustained me.
We have made something beautiful together.

the long slow courage
it takes to make a life -
no cheering crowds

CONTENTS

Start With Things 1
Two Rivers 2
On Discovering the William Stafford Online Archive 3
Suizoku 4
An Ancient Allegory 5
Tea Ceremony 6
Climbing the Mountain 7
What the Old Man Said..8
Love's Limits 10
Like Pressed Flowers 11
No Show 12
Erato Returns after an Unexplained Absence 13
A Rubric on Time 14
Evening Raga for the Suburbs 15
Nocturne...16
The Hand 18
The Old Ones 19
Lost Clouds 20
Love and Fear..21
Haiku Set 1 22
Cages 25
Unasked, Unanswered 26
A Brief Lesson on the Human Experience 28
At the Tomb of the Unknown Poet 29
At the Bimhuis Tram Stop 30
An Open Letter to Gaia 31
Lux perpetua: four octets for my son......................................32
When He Was Twelve 34
Ikaros 36
More About Axe Handles 37
Flight Check 38
The Seed 39
Shakyamuni's Road 40
The Robe...41
The End of Sleep 42

Day of Remembering 44
Love Letter to My Left Hand 45
Wondering Aloud to William Stafford 46
Waves 47
Should Things Become Blurred 48
Different Advice on Death..49
Mr. Death...50
Cosmology 52
Tip of the Iceberg 53
We Interrupt This Reading ... .54
Haiku Set 2 55
Infinity Minus One 58
Walking on the Beach 60
What a Mockingbird Says..61
When the Student is Ready......................................62
Fountain of Age..63
Perspective...64
Creation 65
Incarnation...66
Remembering Dreams..67
A Poem for Darwin Day 68
Signals..69
Cold..70
Speaking of Mountains 71
The Hunt...72
Among the Blind 73
The Hinge 74
Two Trees 76
Gratitude...77
The Remembered Thorn...78
Flowers Without Borders 79
Six Garden Tanka...80
A Song for the Winter Garden 82
Benediction...83
For Kathy...84
Haiku Set 3 85
Heard in the Kitchen 88
Moon Moths...90
Game Face..92
Names...93

Sun Salutation 94
Fetal Position..95
Sabi-Wabi 96
Notes on Selected Poems 98

PREFACE AND ACKNOWLEDGMENTS

Looking back over my life, I see three things as having provided the greatest joy during the good times and the greatest consolation during the hard times: my love of music, my love of poetry, and raising a son with a remarkable woman ideally suited to be his mother. All three have begotten themes in this collection of my poems. Naturally, these three things are not disconnected, and my poems sometimes explore the way they flow together in my experience.

Many, if not all, of these poems are also born out of my lifelong search for meaning, for a place to stand in the headlong rush of life's experiences. This search was first given a particular shape by the strong religious convictions of my family, and this early experience so shaped my thinking and my imaginal world that the language, thought forms, and metaphors that come naturally to me as a poet are often those of the Biblical tradition.

Over the course of my life the search has taken many other forms. I found myself in midlife ready to question the search itself and drawn to the robustly skeptical *via negativa* of Siddhatha Gotama, the Sage of Shakya, whose own long search led him resolutely away from metaphysical speculation and toward a pragmatic way of life where all of life's experience serves the greater goal of cultivating compassion, wisdom, and peace in oneself and one's relations. This shift is also reflected in the poems collected here.

In February, 2011, I was diagnosed with ALS (Lou Gehrig's Disease), a terminal neuro-degenerative disease that leaves one increasingly paralyzed and for which there is no treatment. This inescapable reminder of my mortality is responsible for the many poems here on themes of death and disability. I was very fortunate at the time of my diagnosis to already have a spiritual discipline that encouraged me to take in the inevitability of my own decline and death as not only a part of life, but also a motivation for practice.

I write, in part, because I am inspired to do so by reading

and studying the marvelous poems of others: Whitman, Wordsworth, Cummings, Wendell Berry, Gary Snyder, Robert Bly, Naomi Shihab Nye, Jane Hirshfield, Robin Chapman, Thich Nhat Hanh, and, above all, William Stafford. These are my teachers; I only wish I were a better pupil.

The haiku in this collection come from a ten year period during which I wrote no free verse poems, putting my energies instead into a deep study of the Japanese haiku tradition and the literary English haiku tradition it inspired. Many of the haiku included here were published in the *World Haiku Review, Hermitage, Gong!, The Daily Yomiuri*, and other haiku publications. Among my many mentors and publishers during this period, I owe special thanks to Susumu Takiguchi , Eiko Yachimoto, Ion Codrescu, Norman Darlington, and the late John Carley.

I have included, as a help to the reader, an appendix with notes on many of the poems. The others will, I hope, be self-explanatory.

I am grateful to Ramya Ramaswamy, Sue Cozart, and Kathy Snyder for much-needed help with the manuscript. Nicholas Pippins found the perfect cover art from his photography portfolio and generously gave his permission to use it. Thanks to Karl Snyder, Kathy Snyder, Jinji Willingham, David Zuniga, Donna Bryant Goertz, Robin Chapman, Elise Huneke-Stone, and members of the Friday Poetry List for feedback and discussions of specific poems.

I am always happy to hear from readers at jsnyder@pobox.com. More poems and videos of readings can be found at my website, ordinarypersonslife.com.

John Snyder
Austin, Texas

Start With Things

start with things – not with ideas
things will not betray you:
everything wants to help a beginner

there is more spiritual power
in the fragrance of one rose in your garden
than in all the incense in India

study each thing as if it were
a lost volume of Dante – the one that
told what lay beyond Paradise

sooner or later things will begin
to sing to you, and much later
you will begin to hear their chords

you may want to know if you yourself
are a thing with its own chord –
your knowledge of roses may save you

Two Rivers

Two ancient rivers meet in my heart –
one dark and muddy,
the other crystal-clear.
I swim in the turbulent mystery
born of their great collision.

Maybe there is a shore
beyond joy and despair,
and maybe I will reach it.
Maybe this pathless path leads
to a homeless home
in a city without walls
where gold is not on the streets
but in the hearts of the people.

For now, any hope of progress
requires my full awareness,
arms, legs, lungs, mind,
stroke after stroke pressing
against the current.

On Discovering the William Stafford Online Archive

I have many fathers
for no man can father
a whole boy –
a boy being something
that goes beyond
mere upbringing
or any borders
a father can patrol.

My fathers are many,
as I am many;
they stand spread out
along the road of my life,
some behind me,
their light throwing
my long shadow forward
into the future;

others ahead
waiting, beckoning,
ready to smile
and bless me
as I pass.

Suizoku

He stands quite still, watching the koi weave orange designs in the pond. On the ground beside him is the fish kite he made himself. Eight years ago, leaving protected waters, he began the long upstream swim to where I am, and beyond. In the strong current of my will he leaps and dives, slips out of sight and reappears with a shout and a silver spray of laughter. In the warm wind of my love, like a kite he rises. Already he has pulled far away. I play out the line, and he ascends -- the wind is very strong now. I wait by the water and remember the wetness of cloud-wind upon my own face.

An Ancient Allegory

The ground beneath us has turned to air.
We are borne aloft by shifting winds
of change and chance. Each bound to each
and to the ten-thousand things by gossamer strands
of choice and cause, we are pulled this way and that,
sluggish drifters in Brownian motion, culture-bound.
Many, rejecting even the evidence of their senses,
insist the ground is still somewhere below.
Their legs move in macabre imitations of walking;
they draw illusory lines in sand that isn't there.
Others have grown wings and learned to fly.
We see them soaring high above dawn,
laughing, calling to each other, "How beautiful!
Come and see!" and "Over here –
an ancient road through the jungle!"

Tea Ceremony

Set out cup (howling black wolf
on gray glaze, handmade by Montana friend
Greg Jahn, 1989, or fierce red topeng mask
on white ceramic, Asian Art Museum,
San Francisco, 2010).

Heat fresh, filtered water almost to a boil.
Remove from heat.
Measure two teaspoons loose green tea
(Longjing Dragonwell, Zhejiang Province,
or a good sencha) into tea brewing basket.
Fill cup with hot water;
immerse tea brewing basket.
Steep for three minutes. Serve.

Follow each of these steps as though
it were the most precious thing in the world,
a secret given to you alone
to keep alive in the world.
So much more than a cup
of tea is at stake.

You may have heard that the world
is a battleground of ideas and ambitions;
that to gallop into this fray,
teeth bared, sword flashing,
is the proper use of the mind.
But most days are made of small moves
and life is made of days.

Climbing the Mountain

Scant clouds, the smell of spruce and water:
Today we are climbing the mountain.
People of the coast, our hands are clever,
our eyes are made for distance.
But today the mountain is teaching us
about legs, about lungs. All day,
in the eloquence of its silence
it is speaking to our hearts about wings.

In the evening we rest --
not speaking, but not alone.
Tomorrow, the return
to tamer ground, to familiar paths;
but now we know beyond forgetting:
on the right mountaintop,
anyone can be transfigured.

What the Old Man Said

I met an old man dragging a long sack.
He said *Do you know what's in this sack?*
No I said. *Nor do I care.*
Then I will tell you he said.
St. Peter's cathedral,
sixteen yards of Irish lace,
a fifth of cheap whiskey,
a German pistol, circa 1943,
a baby's blanket, blue,
a Social Security card,
a pair of steel-toed boots,
a boy's jacket, one arm missing,
Senator Joseph McCarthy,
a woman's ring, the stone gone,
three dollars, forty-seven cents, Canadian,
a little scrimshaw statue of the god Priapus,
the blow-off valve from a North Sea oil rig,
the pelt of a harp seal,
the mustache of Augusto Pinochet,
a Turkish prayer rug,
a parachute that won't open,
the liver of Prometheus ...
That's enough I said. *Let me by.*

Wait he said. *Do you know the difference*
between you and me?
The difference between you and me
I said *is that you're a crazy old man*
with a bag full of trash
nothing to do
and no thought for the future
beyond which bridge
you'll sleep under tonight.

No he said.
The difference between you and me
is that I know
what's in my sack
and I'm not ashamed
to tell you.

Love's Limits

Love is a snare.
What we love limits us
unless we also love
what has no limit.
Then we ourselves
are the limit
and our very loving
becomes a prayer
for freedom.

So let us be snared together.
Let our cries join
the groaning of the world
like rain falling at sea.
Let us be free
from freedom's fantasies
like two larks
disappearing together
into
the night
sky.

Like Pressed Flowers

I.

Long ago I saved in a book,
like pressed flowers, the only smile
you ever gave me. Wanting
to see it once more, I open
to the page and find only dust
and memories. My hungry eyes
fall on these lines:
>We must lend ourselves to others
>and give ourselves only to ourselves.

II.

Two young hominids, buried together,
matching necklaces of scored shell
around their necks. We know they used
tools, felt love, had a sense of ritual.
Their friends who buried them
and the slow, impartial processes of Earth
have granted their fondest wish: to become,
like pressed flowers, almost inseparable,
almost one.

No Show

Some mornings I go to the usual meeting place, but no poems come. I wait, picking lint off my sweater or obsessively adjusting the ritual objects. I imagine a little boy at the zoo, scanning the newly refurbished ursine habitat in vain for any sign of the bear. Some days I can hear him grumbling and knocking around backstage; other days: total silence, leaving me to speculate. He's asleep. He's feeling shy today. There's something wrong with him – he's sick. They've quarantined him away from the other animals. He's not here – they've had to airlift him to the zoo in San Diego, the only place that knows how to treat his rare disease. He's dead, and they're not telling anybody. He killed his keeper last night, and they have him locked up while they consult the police and the public relations people. He's escaped! For years he was only pretending he couldn't get across that moat and climb the wall to freedom. Giving up, I throw the sack of peanuts at the pigeons and trudge on into my day, restless, catching a faint scent of betrayal, like the new aftershave that, contrary to the confident promises of the strong-jawed young NASCAR driver in the Superbowl ad, utterly failed to get the girl.

Erato Returns after an Unexplained Absence

After years the door opened.
A bell spoke in the temple,
the walking meditation began again.
I wanted to welcome you—
not without some reserve.
Not too fast. Not too fervent.

Not that my hand much missed
your perfumed touch, my ear
your whispered invitations.
When you left so suddenly,
my desire opened out
into a new shape, also lovely.
The hand of my wanting
quietly formed a new mudra.

Not that I would send you away
since you have returned.
Patience has made me
a father, a husband, a friend.
A man who will neither pursue you,
nor prevent you,
nor fail to listen daily
for the bronze echo
of your approaching laughter.

A Rubric on Time

Time is a tightrope
stretched between the poles
of wanting and not wanting.

Start at either end.
Slowly make your way
to the other end.
Turn and return.
Repeat indefinitely.
After some number of turns
you will fall.
That's the end of it.

In the meantime, some say
learn to walk the rope without fear.
Some say stop in the middle,
balance there, don't look down.

The mystics say
Jump! Jump!

Evening Raga for the Suburbs

I am looking for the beauty in your life,
that clear radiance that St. Francis and the Buddha
could find in anything, anyone.

I know it is there, hidden
in the jungle of possessions
your darkness has cultivated around itself.

It's waiting for you to take something,
anything, into your heart foolishly,
without thought of gain or safety.
Then that beauty I am looking for will flash out,
startling you like a brilliant moth shaken
from an old sweater:
fluttering, shimmering, circling
as though your life were a candle.

It only wants to show you
the gift that is for all of us,
that is possessed by none of us,
that always and everywhere
opens itself to us
in the joyous life,
the loving stars.

Nocturne

At night he would open
the bedroom window,
let the warm air,
redolent of mimosa and juniper,
caress him to sleep.

Returning to the animal body,
he would sniff along the bank,
wind ruffling his fur,
sinews stretching toward
an urgent meeting
with hidden things.

He was a feeling
moving through the body of earth
toward an opening onto
infinite traceries of scent,
olfactory landscapes as vast
as the austral plains.
He was a scarlet unseen joy
running to meet all things
with a ravenous welcome.

He ran silently then, visiting
smooth old places that had always
been the same, new places
that came forward only to him.

Sometimes she would come to him –
the Wolf Mother with shining teeth
and bottomless eyes. Together
they would hunt for what had life
down deep in meat and bone.

In the morning he would remember
only that there had been a place once
where he belonged, a place
too vast, too near
even to have a name.

When he spoke of it at all,
he would call it "a place
where I once lived."

The Hand

Root of the infinitely branching
tree of the mind,
the hand that reaches, grasps,
takes for its own.

Bruised fruit falls
to the forest floor.
Does something older than
hand and mind
and less undone by choice
come quickly to feast
on fruit forever lost?

What will we do then
with the unlived parts of our lives?
The hand can hold
only so much.

The Old Ones

In the end there was only the land,
lonely without the people it had known.

The wind still came to dance the old
dances, but went away disappointed.

The rains gathered, searched each arroyo
for broken twigs, charcoal, any faint sign.

The rocks sent back whatever they heard,
waiting to catch laughter that never came.

The moon climbed up high every night,
looking for someone to sing her a hymn.

The antelope wandered where they willed,
generations without the hunter's scent.

Only the river shrugged its shoulders,
"A world? What is that? It flows on, flows on..."

Lost Clouds

I have seen the cloud people wandering
in the lost places of the air,
staggered across the sky
like the footprints of a blind god,
dark clouds struggling toward the horizon,
dragging shrouds of rain across
the astonished earth.

A life can wander like that,
drifting in the winds
toward a receding horizon.
Little betraying movements –
a crooked step, a forgotten turn,
the imperceptible veer of years –
this is how we follow lost clouds to that place
of forgotten destinations, that desert
of intentions leached away
by great distance.

Love and Fear

I am nineteen.
I am standing in a bookstore in London.
I am panicked, holding my breath, my heart pounding.
I watch the panic slowly pull my hand away from the shelf.

Because there on the shelf, surrounded
by beautiful, sweet-smelling books,
is a serpent about to strike. I almost touched it:
Bertrand Russell's *Why I Am Not a Christian*.

Because my faith is a form of fear.
Because this fear is not properly mine,
but something entrusted to me for safekeeping
by those who love me.
Because deep down I know the serpent
is not in a book, but coiled around my fear.
Because I sense that love of this precious world
casts out fear of the next, and I must choose.

Still trembling, I head for the door
and out into the clement summer night.

Haiku Set 1

hermitage
far across the lake
someone is singing

oars at rest
the crescent moon spills one star
into the ocean

rain on the sidewalk
same sound as
rain on the mountain

the planet spinning
through darkness toward days
full of sunshine

spring cleaning
I find the key to the house
we no longer share

estate sale –
a half-finished canvas
of a perfect rose

ripples
where the cormorant's wing
touched the water

Milky Way above –
flat on our backs
in the wet grass

noon comes softly
through the open windows
along with flies

swirl of the classroom –
on a child's steady hand,
a butterfly dries its wings

silence
sound of the wind chime
silence

                    unable to walk
                    on the beach – I become
                    the ocean instead

a thousand rivers
flow into this ocean
lifting the little boats

Cages

Wherever you find a cage, open it;
whatever was imprisoned, embrace it –
yes, despite its anger, its despair, its fear –
for the essence of a cage is not confinement,
but separation. Every wall, every row of bars
defines two cages, and many a cage
is as invisible as the mind.

Realize no separation, and confinement
can never be a cage. This is how
Laozi could write
    You can know the universe
    without leaving your house.

If a cage will not open,
stay with the prisoner.
Sing until each of you has learned
all the songs the other knows.
Put your face close to the bars;
feel the living breath before the kiss.

Unasked, Unanswered

Yet man is born unto trouble,
as the sparks fly upward. Job 5:7

The skies in my little hometown
were impossibly wide, but not too high.
God needed to stay close, pursuing
his tireless project of marking
our every act, word, and thought.
We weren't the questioning sort.

The men we knew who grew anything
grew cotton, alfalfa, sorghum,
summer watermelons, maybe hay.
Their weatherbeaten faces looked wiser
than they were, but they were no fools.
Only one man in town grew flowers –

I remember perfect roses just the height
of a child's nose, and coxcomb's sinuous
crimson ruffles, open-hearted lantana,
and tough little bachelor's buttons.
(Mama, are these buttons? What's a bachelor?)
When our neighbor wasn't tending his flowers,

I could find him in the cool darkness
of his garage workshop, tending his tools.
His slow smile and the savory smell
of wood, mold, and machine oil
would welcome me into his solitude.
If I didn't ask too many questions,

I could watch him sharpening his spades
and shears. With spinning stone,
a little oil, and a shower of sparks,

26

he could put an edge on steel
as sharp as his wife's tongue.
Questions linger for me still

about those times. To what trouble
was he born, this quiet rose-fancier
with the slow smile and skillful hands?
I see him clearly sitting at his wheel
smiling sadly to himself and to me
as the sparks fly upward.

A Brief Lesson on the Human Experience

What will you have to drink?
Have you heard about our specials?
Do you know what you want?
Sorry, we're out of that.
How spicy would you like it?
Anything else for you?
You can pay me now or pay
up front when you leave.

At the Tomb of the Unknown Poet

> *"A poem is a serious joke, a truth*
> *that has learned jujitsu."* - Wm. Stafford

Balanced there to receive the attack
of the oncoming light, you failed to see
the night creeping up from behind.
One last ill-timed joke you didn't catch.

Thumbing through lit reviews at the bookstore,
I turn first to the biographies,
looking for some hint of your history.
I see you were a surgeon, a truck driver,
a mother, a lawyer, a longshoreman,
even a professor. I look at everyone
differently now.

Your epitaph:
> Serious Fool,
> Scent Follower,
> Sensei of Sense,
> Pearl Diver,
> Poet without Portfolio,
> No-Collar Worker,
> Humane Being.

Mightier than the sword – yes.
But those who live by the pen
shall die by the pen, or,
rarely, (but it does happen),
are caught up alive like Elijah
in heaven's fiery chariot,
never to be unseen again.

At the Bimhuis Tram Stop

alone at the tram stop
this raw spring night
my body tired but alive
after hours of jazz
currents splitting and joining into
waves of darkness and light
neither gaining the upper hand
far down the straight track
along Piet Heinkade
the headlight of the last tram
although I could walk
to the train station from here
to ride almost alone at midnight
in this miraculous moving
chamber of light toward my little
room near the Diamond Bridge
spent and full is the greatest happiness
the doors open
and I enter

An Open Letter to Gaia

They say you may die
if we keep living this way.
What am I to do
with this information?
In the mockingbird's songs
now I hear a silent spring.

Or I hear Rube Goldberg laughing:
just push this shiny gold button
on my Industrial Age Machine and
three hundred years later
your cities float away.

Gaia, I got your message –
the more helpful one
you so kindly left
in the diamond-bright web
of the orb-weaver,
each connection carefully made
according to the ancient pattern,
the whole defiantly anchored
to a tire, the sidewalk,
and my car door.

I stood still with my hand
on the door handle, reading
the message over and over.
When I understood,
I went back inside
and wrote you a poem
instead.

Lux perpetua: four octets for my son

I.

I knew the summery night of your beginning.
I knew the winter darkness of your becoming.
Struggling into my blessed and blessing hands
your bruised head and bloody shoulders came
that night of your presentation to the light.
Between your mother and me a region
of uncharted heaven opened, slowly turning
bright constellations around your polar star.

II.

With all the intensity in my scholar's heart
I have studied the amber lightplay in your eyes,
the poignant symmetry of your shoulder blades,
the patient, open way you watch a friend,
the way you think before you speak, or cry, or laugh.
Karl, just the way your hair lies curled upon
your temples is a thing so ineffably right
as to stun the jaded philosopher into silence.

III.

Living far ahead into our future,
I know the dark potential you inherit –
the folly, misplaced passion, fear, and cunning
that leave a lucky man with something better
and rob another man of all his birthright.
You hold one end of the rope; I hold the other.
Karl, we can bind up death! Or make
a noose to choke your future and my past.

IV.

One fact I wear as an amulet against despair:
between the nested parentheses of perception,
one could never hope to bracket one scintilla
of the flaming light you carry in your body.
When we are quiet together in the evening,
beyond the pallid saying and doing of the day,
I humbly take off my shoes and let that burning
cast my shadow on ancient holy ground.

When He Was Twelve

When he was twelve, so was I,
though thirty years had passed
since I was twelve when he was not.

That first twelve, the mirror was full
of my face. I hoped that only I saw
fear flicker in my eyes, tightness
guard the corners of my mouth
around soft, full lips (they called
me nigger, for there were no blacks
in our school for them to hate). I wished for
and practiced a harder look,
while early pimples like little sunspots
came and went on my too-broad
forehead. Taciturn and wary
around the others – big, rough boys
with older brothers, and fathers
who came home from the oil fields
dog-tired and spoiling for a fight.

These boys knew blunt-edged words
I only pretended to understand:
pissing match, bench press, faggot,
goddamyoufuckingworthlesslittleshit.
They sat in loveless clumps after school
and grinned as I walked home alone,
struggling with my load of books
and my shiny new violin case.
Hey, nigger! Hey, piss-ant!
I looked straight ahead, careful
to keep a steady pace.

When he was twelve, so was I.
We joined hands and strode out
to enjoy the world, laughing and easy,

34

this sunny boy and I, when he was twelve,
and we had nothing to fear.

Ikaros

What if we changed the story, had some sadistic god
bestow upon Ikaros the gift of acrophobia.
He'd stand, trembling, on the edge of the cliff,
his wild young body longing to give itself
to unbounded space and rapturous ascent —
his soul by chains of fear as grimly tethered to the rock
as Prometheus ever was.

What then? If we run the tale ahead,
say, fifty years, would we find him
still there on Crete, for decades fatherless;
light-filled wings now withered arms?
What bitterness or loss would his neighbors
read in his eyes or his poems? Or
would he have found other means of ascent
not driven by hot blood and young muscle,
but by the slow fermentations of desire —
or maybe by flinging himself
around the great orb of his fear,
as a comet is swept around the sun
and shot again into the void?

Or would we find him safe in Samos,
surrounded by his flocks and grandchildren?
"There were difficult times and wings repeatedly lost,
but I was saved by my mother, the king's concubine,
who came in a dream to say,
        'Look, Ikaros, at my life
        and understand as your father never did:
        one does not reach the heavens
        by flying — but by falling.'"

More About Axe Handles

In "Axe Handles" Gary Snyder cites Ezra Pound:
>*When making an axe handle,*
>*the pattern is not far off.*
The father and son make the axe together
that it may be wielded long years for good, not ill.
But when the handle is finished,
there remains the securing of it
to the axe – no easy task.
How will the blade be sharpened?
Surely by rock harder
than the heart of any father.

Flight Check

These boys are getting ready to fly.
You can see the secret in their eyes,
in a sudden lightness of gait,
in a new set of the shoulders,
a broadening of the chest
from the weight of wings.
They are drawn to racing;
when they run, one can almost see
the flock skimming low over the water
before rising in formation.
They watch each other carefully
for answers: are you the one,
the first of us to hear the call,
the one who will step into the air
and be gone? Am I?

The Seed

See the
seed a
seething
thing see
how its
hour true
light from
light is
opening

inert in
earth a
mystery
unfolds
unseen
enfolds a
sacred
seam of
energy

a part
apart yet
All-sprung
springs
and grows
unsung
in sun
o sing
alleluia!

Shakyamuni's Road

What can I tell them?
I looked hard at the world,
and it looked back at me
with my own face.
I told this story to my friends;
now they look everywhere
for my face

All my life I tried to help them —
these worshipers, they bend my words
into grapple hooks to fling into the sky,
thinking by determination to climb
hand over hand out of the hell realms

They clutch my teachings, their knuckles
white with grim gratitude
      keys, they say, *our teacher has given us keys*
      to unlock 84,000 Dharma doors
      we vow to unlock them all

Only Mahakashyapa
heard the true sermon
in the silences between my words
      where there is no wall, there cannot be a door
      where there is no door, there is nothing to unlock
      open the hand of belief and see:
      the road I traveled
      leads everywhere

The Robe

Born *in media res* in a story
with no beginning and no end

> *All I have in this world:*
> *a robe, a bowl, a needle with a little thread*

What I thought was stillness
is everything moving in complete harmony

> *From scraps of cloth no one wants*
> *this robe is sewn to keep an old monk warm*

No matter how strong the storm,
what floats continues to float

> *From my teacher's hands I received this robe;*
> *his arm always around my shoulder*

The vastness seeps into my bones,
making them as light as a bird's

> *When this robe is all new patches,*
> *is it still my robe?*

A bit of cloth torn
from an unknown tapestry

> *So many relics of the Buddha's robe:*
> *they could clothe the whole Sangha!*

Dissolving in laughter
the great question of birth and death

The End of Sleep

The body being still and wanting nothing,
the mind searches the great labyrinth
it has made for itself. Restlessly, it opens
door after door onto rooms it once built, inhabited
for a second or a year, and abandoned. Rooms
completely bare; rooms oddly furnished,
full of curiosities; rooms like the halls of
great museums mysteriously abandoned
by visitors and curators alike. Always
the mind searches, driven on by the lash
of its great loneliness, longing
for something, anything, that it is not –
sometimes up narrow staircases, the air heavy
with stale odors of cooking and unwashed laundry,
sometimes surprised by trapdoors, plunging,
dizzy and terrified, into rooms full of light
or rooms of Plutonian darkness. At length
it opens a door, unmarked and unremarkable
as all the others, that enters not onto a room,
but onto a summer night. Exultant, the seeker
walks out into an open starlit field, heart expanding,
welcomed by the millions of living things
and rocks and oceans and sky and...
and loneliness standing there, much chastened,
but bearing in its eyes the unwelcome message
       this too, all this, alas,
       is but your own face
       before you were born.

Freed from hope, having nowhere else to go,
the seeking mind sits down under a tree to wait
for something to come to it on the breeze,
anything at all that is not of its own making.

See, it waits there still, while the Morning Star
breaks free of the trees, spilling its light
into the darkness – light as of a distant door
opening onto morning and the end of sleep.

Day of Remembering

On the memorable fields of this world,
long stems of sweet grass bow down
heads heavy with seed. Promises
of the next spring hang trembling
in a sulphurous breeze. Crushed
suddenly by boot or knee
or bleeding chest, pressed
into earth's darkness, seeds dream
of children who will never be born
to wander these fields.

In the hearts of politicians,
seeds of fear, greed, ambition
sprout, effloresce in thickets
of tangled justification,
curl tripping tendrils
around young men's legs.

The running,
the shooting,
the falling.
The prick and smell of wet grass.
The last sudden memory
of childhood holidays,
wrestling brothers on the lawn,
the grown-ups drinking sugared tea,
telling glorious tales of the Big War.
The remembering, then
the darkness,
the darkness.

Love Letter to My Left Hand

Rest here in my lap; your work is almost done.
See, you can cradle my right hand in meditation –
a fitting end for such a spiritual seeker as you.

Right-handed as I am, you played second fiddle
as I took hold of life. But when I picked up my violin,
ah, then you were the concertmaster of the body's orchestra.
Everything depended on you, on your strength, your agility,
your sensitivity, your ardor.

Do not think because you are weak and weakening
I do not love you. This alloy of compassion
for what you are, memories of what you were,
and loss of what you might have been –
surely, it is a kind of love.

I shall never forget that you were once
magnificent and generous of spirit.
When I gave up the violin for the viola,
you humbly became a beginner again,
letting go of hard-won habit
and pride of accomplishment.

How happy you were in those days,
becoming the hand of Bartok or Brahms,
Vaughn Williams or Debussy!
Your joy filled my whole body.
Now you want to curl into a fist
that never opens, but I will not let you.
Your future is openness,
becoming the one hand that silently claps
at the moment of awakening.

Wondering Aloud to William Stafford

I went online to buy your book
A Scripture Of Leaves, now out-of-print.
Twelve used copies, the cheapest one
a hundred more dollars than I could spend.
I gazed at the cover a long, deep time,
remembering a poem that lay beneath.
But a hundred dollars is a month of meds,
a day of care, a doctor's time.

Two leaves were on the cover etched:
Are they falling or holding on?
The scripture they carry, how's it compare
with medical scrip, a doctor's advice?
Do we heal by letting go,
gracefully falling when autumn comes?
Am I a leaf, a tree, a book
of scriptures left unread, unpenned?

Do we live by holy words?
Or not by words but by the paired
pirouettes of heart and mind
lively at first, then spiraling down
to rest at last on genial earth,
to nourish roots of deeper things
than poems, pills, and prophecies?

Waves

What is the shape of a wave?
That is my shape,
a brief swelling on the surface—
my deepest thoughts,
my care, my projects,
all spindrift in the wind.
Do not say that I
came into the world,
lived a little while,
and returned to my source.
See the wind-driven froth
for what it is, dive deep.
Say, instead, no world to enter,
no one to enter it,
no life to live,
no death to die,
no source to leave or return to.
Say I am the ocean
taking the shape of a wave,
surrounded by limitless waves,
swelling out of that greatest wave,
the tide - incalculable power
breathing in, breathing out
forever.

Should Things Become Blurred

Should things become blurred
by a brain dissolving, a mind
slowly letting go of itself,
may it be a beautiful blurring,
as on nights around the Christmas tree
when a nearsighted boy, glasses off,
could lose himself in a world awash
in softly blending orbs of color,
or like London lights unfocusing
toward each other on a foggy night.

Should the sharp edges between events
begin to fade, event joining event
in a seamless tapestry of time,
may it be an oceanic fading,
as raindrops join a river joining an ocean,
or as receding waters reveal
an archipelago to be a mountain range.

Should words break rank
and wander bravely on their own
or travel obliquely as groups of strangers,
may they be loved for who they are –
world makers, songs without melodies –
no longer implements in the mind's
wolfish conquest of the world.

Should things become blurred,
I pray you let go of sense, of fear, of pity,
if they will not stand aside for love.

Different Advice on Death

Take no advice from poets playing Peter Pan,
but as a man return death's gaze with bravest calm
and never blink.

Though life be wise or wild, no raging near the end
will extend one's time a whit, nor lead the watching
young to wisdom.

Greet death with proffered hand and steady smile,
but know the while that death and life are blinkered readings
of one fiction.

In truth, the light we cast in living never dies;
it ramifies. It shines for good or ill through countless
generations.

Mr. Death

I who would be a friend to all confess
I hold you, Mr. Death, in sad contempt.

How tiresome your sophomoric pranks,
your arm suddenly around my throat,
your bony, unwashed hand over my eyes;
your meaningless hooting and gibbering
into the silence of a prayer; the way
you commandeer the stage of my body,
simpering and strutting
through your tiresome kabuki play
of aches and pains, alarms and failures.

One might almost take compassion
on you, the ugly, boorish little bully
nobody wants to play with,
but I fear, Mr. Death, these fine sentiments
would be lost on you, so devouring
is your desire to dominate, so desperate
your need to have the last word.
Even when you close the eyes
of the suffering and we are glad,
even then, we see through your crocodile tears
and begrudge you such easy victories.

The wisest among us bearded you ages ago.
Even I, blind as a bat and squinting into
the dim, smoky cabaret I call a mind,
see you for what you are: a scarecrow
dressed up in tatters of my discarded dreams,
stuffed with the dusty straw of superstition
and childhood terrors never comforted.

In a clear mind's mirror, you cast no reflection;

you are gone in the light of understanding
like a breath on a cold day. As my ashes
prepare to scatter themselves into the wind,
not even a shadow of you falls on anything real.

Cosmology

every mind a universe
billions upon billions

each vast and expanding
full of immeasurable

energies of death and life
each receiving faint

signals from the others
perturbations in

the field of consciousness
constantly birthing

new universes
each randomly winking out

in a few nano-eons
only the faint signals

transduced a trillion ways
whisper-like, remain

Tip of the Iceberg

A long, violent birth it was,
being pushed farther and farther
off the continent, hanging on
as long as I could—then a fracture line
racing across the glacier and I sliding
catastrophically into the waves.

Glad, glad I was then to hide
my immensity out of sight—
if I could I would have sunk entirely
to hide my consternation, my loneliness.
Eventually, I came to love this life

as a seaborne free-agent, an icy
intimidation to any approaching ship,
terrifying in my solitude
and in the implications
of my frosty indifference.

Once, I thought that depth
and hidden substance
were my defining marks,
but now the constant melting
seems more to the point.

For a while I didn't know if I
were the iceberg or the ocean,
but now I see (and it is the end
of isolation) that I am the iceberg
becoming the ocean becoming the
iceberg again and again and again.

We Interrupt This Reading ...

Quick! Free yourself!
That wasn't a poem I just gave you—
it was a diamond-tipped hacksaw
for the bars of your heart.

Hurry! Right now
I am distracting the guards
with a little verbal juggling
and poetic sword swallowing—
any minute they may catch on
and return with a vengeance.

Go! Make a break for it!
Rumi still waits in that field of his.
I've been there—we can find the way.

Haiku Set 2

in my son's pocket
my hand finds a stone
smoothed by ancient seas

father and son
descend into a canyon
older than language itself

leaving the school
each salmon seeks the source
of its own stream

fiftieth spring:
early daffodils
still surprise me

bowing to others
he shows his greatest beauty -
winter sunset

the sound of the bell
in the air – the mind in
the sound of the bell

candlelight
all I can see is
Kuan Yin's smile

this old shoulder
can't chop wood, carry water,
or hold up the world

the long slow courage
it takes to make a life -
no cheering crowds

I sip tea and see
the Buddha's hand
lifting the cup

how happy for us
jasmine traded its color
for this fragrance

funeral cortege
terrifying pure white
of the apple blossoms

Infinity Minus One

Strong Hall, 1984.
This professor, my favorite,
holds the chalk sideways,
like the bow of a cello,
filling the blackboard
with mathematical runes.

Through the window, blue Kansas sky;
my mind is caught by something
she said a few minutes ago.
I struggle to get a purchase on
infinity minus one is still infinity.

She says don't try to interpret it,
don't give it meaning it doesn't have;
it's beyond experience –
just accept it as one
of many unlikely truths
that follow inexorably
from the impersonal axioms of set theory.
I say nothing, but I can't let go of it.

I know this professor sits Zen,
long hours conjuring emptiness,
starting from the axiom of open awareness –
not so different from her daily work
using finite means to explore the infinite.
Not so different from my need to understand.

Thirty years later, I am still caught
by infinity minus one.
Through the window, blue Texas sky;
I work out new corollaries of experience.
When the last poem is written,

an infinity of truths will still be unsaid.
When I am gone, infinity minus one
will still be infinity.

Walking on the Beach

Before me, a shining strip of sea-smoothed shore.
Step after step, my foot pressing into the sand –
the feel of that persisting in my body.
Behind me, a lengthening trail of empty footprints.

Holding these three truths together
is what it means to walk on the beach.

These three and one other:
the certain knowledge that the next tide
will perform the selfless ritual
of beginning anew.

What a Mockingbird Says

If what a mockingbird says
is heard in the right way
by the ear that has also heard
the promise of love long kept
and the long sigh of one grown old
in the century of abandonment,

and if this hearing is taken
into thought in the right way
and held there in a place
that has also long held
a prayer for courage
and the image of any perfect thing,

and if this holding in thought
comes in the right way
to dwell in the heart
that has also been home to
a rich emptiness thicker than blood
and the fertile despair of remorse,

and if what lives in this heart
is breathed out in the right way
past lips that have spoken worlds
into and out of being,

then what had been mute as clay
may stand up enfleshed
and begin to sing its own songs
to any ear that hears
in the right way.

When the Student is Ready

(for William Stafford)

"A life went by, just
a life, no claims."

One of the mockingbird's songs
says that. Another time she says

"The mystery does not get clearer
by repeating the question."

Such as I am,
I repeat the question.

She flys away saying
"Just a life, no claims."

Fountain of Age

Sweet water here.
Old men standing together
    (jade of wisdom,
    granite of endurance,
    sapphire of slow passion)
like rock in the desert.

I strike the rock,
pray Heaven to give me
water for the next
forty years.

Perspective

Some say the sky fell;
I say the earth ascended.
We longed for the Universal,
thoughts that couldn't be soiled
by human experience. Someone
pointed out that thoughts
were also human experience,
and the forensic team found
our fingerprints all over Heaven.
A few suggested we try longing for
thoughts that couldn't be thought,
but there was little consolation in that.
We became nomads again,
each family loyal to its family gods,
no longer sure where we were.
Where were all the sacred hilltops,
smoky from the fires of sacrifice?
Every Here was only here,
and There was only someone else's Here.
Then Descartes pushed his zero-pin
into the map of the universe,
and There appeared everywhere.
We struggled to learn the new map,
squinting at the unshadowed image
of this little blue world
spinning in the harsh light
of its fervid star.

Creation

After chaos, clouds of dust;
from clouds, stars;
from stars, planets and their moons.
On this planet, rivers and oceans,
giving rise to clouds and minds.
If god does not yet exist, this cosmos,
with its clouds of unknowing –
who is to say what it might conceive
in the womb of time?

Incarnation

> *Just to be is a blessing; just to live is holy.*
> *- Abraham J. Heschel*

When I asked my heart,
there was no garish star,
no singing angels,
no breathless shepherds,
no mysterious Magi.

Just the beleaguered father,
the hungry baby,
the exhausted mother:
a family blessed by being,
a child holy because alive.

Remembering Dreams

Some say the trick
to remembering dreams
is to know, when asleep,
that you're dreaming.
It's not that easy:
waking life has all
the marks of a dream,
save the time of waking
and remembering.

Last night I dreamed of water and sky,
an old friend on the far coast and I
staying up all night
remembering dreams.

A Poem for Darwin Day

Poets wonder aloud who made
the bright-burning tiger? Who made
the lamb, the black bear, the grasshopper?
Rhetorical questions perhaps,
but the earth offers in her openhearted
generosity an answer for anyone
with ears to hear: the tiger made herself
from non-tiger elements,
from what she did and when
and where. Likewise, each living thing
makes its future by unmaking the thing
it is, and each living thing
makes all the others in the same way.

How very far from love and wisdom
were the philosophers who thought
the real was in a realm
forever beyond experience.
Our birthright of belonging
to this kaleidoscopic world –
how ingenuously we traded it
for their thin gruel of speculation.

The question what are you?,
the asymptote of what has Earth done?,
has never come close
to a final answer.

Signals

How surpassingly strange,
the fragile signals we send each other:
evanescent tremblings in the air,
light captured on a page in squirms of ink;
microvoltaic movements of muscles
around eyes, forehead, mouth.

Subtle fluctuations of energy flow
from openness to openness,
becoming in turn rich polyphonies,
the clement murmur of contentment,
starless, cataclysmic chords of despair,
or fingernails on the chalkboard of reason.

Listen! The body resounds with intelligence
riding on the nerves, borne by the blood.
Delicate auroras of meaning dance
across the vast distances between atoms.

How surpassingly strange,
these separate selves we think we are —
empty energetic eddies, never-ending,
carried on the field of being, even
to the edge of the expanding All.

Cold

Bits of char in a fire pit,
a gray December drizzle,
shimmering rings of Saturn,
Gary Snyder's bare feet in a mountain stream –
no two things are cold in quite the same way.
Still, we speak of cold as a thing.
We smile and nod when teachers say
there is no cold, just the absence of heat.
Then we go on speaking of absences.
We nudge and wink as these empty nouns
without portfolio squat in places made for things.

My soul grows cold at the thought.

Speaking of Mountains

When Li Po said "mountain"
he meant mountain
and the way the oldest son
stands in the life of the family
and why the emperor's throne
is made of jade
and how a poem can live
six hundred years.

When Dante said "mountain"
he meant the shape of a mountain in the soul
and a solitary climber on it.

When Thomas Mann said "mountain"
he meant Europe lost in a blizzard.

When Lord Russell said "mountain"
he meant mountain.

When Beckett says "mountain"
he means nothing.

I will take my son to look for jade
in the mountains.

The Hunt

It's 3 AM; the great horned owls and I are hunting again.
From my bed I hear their sonorous cries echo
between dark houses. I imagine them
perched on my neighbor's roof, immense
silhouettes of sublime beauty and death,
scanning our garden, our trees, the shadows beyond.

I scan my own moon-dappled field of experience,
obliquely remembered landscapes, darkly contoured
and half-hidden by an early mist
or the smoke of yesterday's dying fires.
Starved for strength and sweetness,
I suck the marrow of memory, bone after bone.

Morning light often reveals
the scattered feathers of a dove –
this ravenous world lives by the hunt,
each hungry creature taking and being taken,
turning in the dance rooted in joy
rooted in grief.

Among the Blind

Sun and moon stand apart in the sky
like quarreling lovers.
No one sees.

Daylight drifts out, beautiful, to sea,
quietly vanishes into dark water.
No one sees.

Crows circle above the house,
wings black enough to swallow the sun.
No one sees.

Among the blind
there is no word
for "shadow."

The Hinge

Would you know what we are?
Consider, then, the artless cruelty of children
and their boundless compassion.

Here is young Terry, fifty years ago in fifth grade.
Here is the teacher looming over him.
Terry, why is your paper
not yet numbered 1 through 10?
What's wrong with you?
Terry, the class is waiting.
Hair uncombed, shoelaces untied,
he rummages for a pencil
in his rat's nest of a desk.
We with the neatly numbered papers
feign impatience and smirk
at his baggy overalls, his mismatched socks.
Inveigling us to see him
through hawkish eyes,
the teacher turns us against him –
no doubt for his good and ours.
On the playground, our games of tag
are ruthless rituals of separation:
he is always *It.* To be touched by him
is to join him in his defilement.
So desperate is he to join our games,
he often starts them himself,
wearing the pariah's crown of thorns
we have woven him from our fear.
(*And yet* –
we sense the source
of true defilement, bleed
from the wounds we give.)

What we were then, we still are:

impossible beings, moral chimeras,
aggregates of jangling need
in a jumble of urges so tangled
we shrug and call it choice.
Where there should be a spine,
we find a hinge
and a door swinging freely
between malice and mercy.

(*And yet* –

Two Trees

All day little brown birds
have come to our leafless tree,
perched for a moment,
then hurried away.
I don't know why they come,
why they chose our tree,
whether they will return.
I cannot fly.

The birds, for their part,
do not know that they are stardust
and that to stardust they will return.
They cannot love me, as I love them,
nor can they hate, enslave, or war.

Perhaps their forebears perched
for a moment in that ancient Tree,
but they moved on quickly,
never pecking at that fruit
that made us human.

Gratitude

Skillful words of my teachers,
you words that were my refuge,
the ladder I climbed to safety,
I bow to you in gratitude,
my forehead touching the ground.

How strong you seemed, how solid
those times I hung between earth
and sky, the wind tearing
at my body, gravity
prying open my fingers.

I could push away the ladder,
let it topple and fall. Instead
I find I want to bow and walk
away, leave the ladder here
for some other fugitive.

The Remembered Thorn

Heart pounding, Androcles knelt
beside the anguished lion, felt
more than heard the rumble in the throat.

Precious little of lions knew he
or how to turn the paw, gently
probe to find and take away the thorn.

Hesitant, but fearing pain
would overcome the lion's restraint,
he despaired – then memories arose.

A rustic boyhood, unshod feet
scrambling over the hills of Crete,
a shortcut through the field, a misplaced step.

Clutching his foot in agony,
turning it over gingerly
to find the wound an inch-long thorn had made.

Then suddenly he was the beast;
the pain was his, resolve increased
as in now-steady hands he grasped the paw.

The lion gave an astonished roar
the thorn was in his paw no more;
the great tongue licked away the drops of blood.

So memory re-vivifies
experience, and we are wise
to seek in it a key to understanding.

The more we see the common core
of lived experience, the more
our suffering serves to heal the other.

Flowers Without Borders

The bluebonnets that last year volunteered
to grow in the garden path (we smiled
at their can-do spirit and let them be)
have this year continued their march
to the gate – *fleurs sans frontieres* – lined up
in blue and white helmets,
stopping us at the checkpoint to deliver
an urgent humanitarian message:
> *Grow your life beyond its borders!*
> *You, too, can make a little progress on the path.*

Six Garden Tanka

I.
the old gardener
cutting roses for
an anniversary bouquet –
his practiced hands
never touch a thorn

II.
would the garden grow
without my long, steady love?
perhaps the question is
would my long, steady love
grow without this garden?

III.
two mockingbirds
square off on the garden path
the garden smiles
and continues its slow stretch
into full awakening

IV.
when Babylon fell
how long did it take the gazelles
to return to its gardens?
too proud to apologize
I distract myself with poems

V.
Orion turns above
the silent, silvered garden
where I look for answers
even dung beetles navigate
by the Milky Way

VI.
time is the river
that flows through this garden
every plant an eddy
I lay down my sweat-stained oars
and let the current take me

A Song for the Winter Garden

Where these lifeless stems are coiled
into the fence, let me not imagine
burgeoning plumbago. Let me see
these blasted stalks and stumps
for what they are, not as ciphers
for sun-bathed salvia, bulbine, and mallow.

These abandoned nests of bird and wasp,
no longer nests, but wintry abstractions –
let joy and wonder arise at the sight of them.
Heaped detritus of life, not yet reborn –
may wisdom arise: subject to decay
are all, yes all, conditioned things.

Let me not prefer these perennials
whose roots sleep soberly in the ground
to the annuals who dazzled then died,
betting the future on something
as uncertain as a seed.

If I cannot welcome this austere harvest
as I welcomed the abundance of spring,
how can I embrace this failing body?
How can I return peacefully to this soil
that is by turns womb and tomb?

Let the silence of this place be an opening,
neither the absence of bee and finch,
nor the cloistering of a life against death.
Carve me in ice; for my heart, leave a little
of the emptiness between the stars.

Benediction

the monks of winter
    have carefully scratched
        the inky skeletons of trees
            onto the parchment sky

the garden is
    as still and full
        as the moment before
            Evensong begins

oblique light
    through cloud prisms
        like sunset through
            a rose window

it is enough now
    to believe in
        what I sense and
            in this winter eve

the birds' empty nests
    preach eloquently
        of leaving behind
            what no longer serves

back inside, the sun's
    last psalm in my heart,
        steady rhythm of
            footsteps on the path

For Kathy

These old photographs you found –
how young we look, how new to love.
Your fresh young face was the answer
to all my questions then.
Now it radiates a different beauty,
an answer to deeper questions.

Like a flagstone on the path
worn smooth by decades
of comings and goings,
our love is long in the making.
All the nights you are too tired
after work to put me to bed,
and you do it anyway –
I lie back and touch the stone:
feeling how smooth it is,
how cool to the touch,
how firmly set in the earth.

That young couple in the photographs –
how tender my heart is for them,
knowing what I know.
If I could, should I warn them
away from the path they are taking?
I look into your loving eyes,
and I have my answer.

Haiku Set 3

wings of youth
melting in the sun
in your arms

        she finds his midnight
        explanations as hazy
        as the spring moon

climbing to the top
of the tallest mountain we see,
we see Everest

        this alpine lake
        another familiar place
        I haven't been

morning dew
in the teacups we left
by the campfire

daggers of sunlight
frame the spiral
on the solstice stone

only mud
at the bottom of our well -
mocking blue sky

this morning
the river has new sandbars -
no news of you

the music of streams
heard again on the mountain
you home from the war

on the flagpole:
a brass eagle and
a mourning dove

newspaper war stories
covered with poems -
calligraphy practice

mourners tell each other
how much he loved his children –
tip of the iceberg

Heard in the Kitchen

I'm sure it was one of the aunts
who said it. Just a few words,
but words so perfectly shaped
for the truth of that world
and so rightly spoken into
the emptiness of the moment
that something opened
for the boy I was, something
about the power of words
to make and unmake worlds,
glimpsed as one might glimpse,
from the window of a train, a gap
in the trees, revealing an ocean
that one had not known was there.

I remember it was one of the aunts
and not the uncles, they being more
about doing than saying, or about
simply sitting and walking together
in silence, letting the hard kernel
of manhood soften and sweetly dissolve
into brotherhood; then when they joined
the women in the kitchen, saying things like
do you remember when...?
or *nobody could hold a candle
to Mama's sweet pickles,*
or *does anybody ever hear from Frank?
I haven't seen him since Daddy's funeral.*

And then, a brother to a sister:
*You know... I sure wish I had been nicer
to you when we were kids.*
And the sister replying, *It's all right.
You weren't half as mean to me*

as your brothers were to you.
Did you get a jar of these
sweet pickles I put up last week?

Moon Moths

In need of wisdom in my life
I go at dusk to the garden
so full of silken shadows,
inner light, a gentle flow
of ephemeral colors,
and the last, quiet visits
of soft-winged creatures.

The twilit garden invites
a wide-angled way of seeing;
the gathering of faint light
from far-distant stars
and the gently swaying grass;
the indirect gaze that sees
hints of coming and going.

Wisdom works its slow way
in the sheltered places to appear
in the bright-skied world
as the impossibly light touch on the arm;
the whisper of a word in the inner ear;
a folded note slipped under
the door of consciousness.

Say you stayed up half the night
watching a pair of moon moths
(their wings spread against the stone wall).
They might never show you
their sudden, silent flight
through moon-silver flowers.

In the morning they would be gone,

but you might just intuit
the powdery imprint of their wings
against the stone
and it would be enough.

Game Face

These masks you see are all I have.
You think I am hiding my true self,
but that is just a conceit of yours,
one of the masks you wear:
Finder of Personal Essences.
You think I'm like an onion,
that layers can be peeled away
to find a marvelous singularity.
A few layers in, can you truly say
one layer is more the onion than any other?
When the last layer is gone,
does your empty hand somehow hold
the True Onion? What part
of this insubstantial Unborn Onion
has Buddha nature?

I was not born what I am;
I have been made by what I do
and what you call a mask is the face
I wear for one of my world-making rituals.
The story goes on and on, masks
changing as needed – now Rama,
now Sita, now Ravana.

Names

Whistling ducks have come to our pond this summer.
Whole families can be seen crossing the road.
They float quietly among the reeds,
looking for bugs, preening their breast feathers.
But never have I heard them whistle.
Names are like that; people mark you
with what's most unusual, not your nature,
not the song you really sing.

Someone sees a shooting star
at the moment of your birth, and you become
Tecumseh, your people's word for that.
Maybe by accident you write one good poem,
and now you are that poet that all your friends know.
You win a race in eighth grade and they
chisel "Sam 'Lightning' Smith" on your tombstone.
Or maybe you become the famous composer
of such-and-such when people inexplicably forget
to ignore one of your hundreds of songs.
Your legs stop working, and now the neighbors
know you as the guy in the wheelchair.

Down at the pond, the ducks and I remain
open to possibilities. Maybe I will hear a whistle;
maybe they will hear a good poem;
maybe we will all be overshot by a streaking star.
Everything we do could be a name;
like God, we could have thousands,
and not one of them would say who we really are.

Sun Salutation

Shakyamuni, should your Middle Way obscure
the wall-breaking beauty of this world,
that has from time to time
in this very life staggered me,
left me strange to myself,
but recognizable in all things,
I cannot follow it.

But I rather think, despite
the pious pallor of your scribes,
that you, Noble Son of the Sun,
awoke to this very ground
of blazing joy at the heart of things.
Indra's net was, for you, no infinity
of icy, crystalline perfection,
but a fabric of immeasurable strength
woven of every cry of wonder,
every praise song ever born
in the throats of living beings.
Your nirvana was not the blowing out
of candles in the darkness, but seeing
clearly their irrelevance to a life
lived in the radiance of true love.

My day begins:
bedside blinds drawn to reveal the Sun,
face turned toward the warmth,
heart and Sun bow to each other, laughing,
as one might bow before a mirror.

Fetal Position

We all start out this way
light as spun glass
almost transparent

Head bowed a little
as if in meditation
or deepest sleep

Delicate, unburdened spine,
tiny ribs flare out
to protect the chest

The untried heart, whole
and ardent for
its two billion beats

Fingers unweb and extend,
open and close,
get ready to hold on

In the warm darkness,
we hear distant voices,
wait for the life-saving push

Thereafter, lightness and transparency
are ideals sought in the heart.
We could all end this way.

Sabi-Wabi

Leery of perfection, the Japanese master
in work of wood or stone or ink leaves
a single flaw that marks the piece
a part of someone's contingent life,
the work of very human hands.

My art, my life, these wild tangles
of flaw stretched over a frame of folly –
I would be content for them to bear
the tiniest marks of perfection,
gentlest knocks on the door of heaven.

Notes on Selected Poems

p. 2 This poem employs a number of metaphors found in the Pali canon, the collection of the oldest texts of Buddhism.

p. 4 "Suizoku" literally means "water beings." To the Japanese, the carp (koi) embodies vital energy and vigor. On Boys' Day, carp kites are flown to celebrate the qualities of strength and perseverance that a boy will need as he "swims upstream."

p. 11   The quote is from Montaigne.

p. 13   Erato was the Greek Muse of lyric poetry.

p. 21   Based on an experience I had in London, 1974. "… perfect love casts out fear." 1 John 4:18 "Clement" has two meanings.

p. 22   English-speaking children are usually taught in school that a haiku is a three line poem with five, seven, and five syllables, respectively. This is a deep misunderstanding of what makes a poem a haiku. The essence of haiku is what Bassho called "haiku spirit", not the counting of syllables. Because of profound differences between Japanese and English, the great majority of English language haiku poets have concluded that it is most respectful to the long tradition of haiku not to observe 5-7-5 when writing in English. For readers interested in learning more about haiku, I recommend the books of Jane Reichhold and William J. Higginson.

p. 26   Based on memories of my childhood in Big Spring, Texas.

p. 30   The Bimhuis in Amsterdam is a world-class venue for jazz and other improvised music. This poem recalls a performance I heard there by Michael Formanek, Craig

Taborn, Tim Berne, and Gerald Cleaver. The music they were playing was later released on the album *The Rub and Spare Change.*

p. 34   Based on memories of my adolescence in Odessa, Texas, contrasted with memories of my son at that age. As children grow up, parents often have the opportunity to reconnect with parts of their own childhood, sometimes with healing results.

p. 40   Regarding the allusion at the end, according to legend, the Buddha once gathered his community and, instead of giving a talk, simply held up flower. Only one of his most advanced students, Mahakashyapa, understood the message and smiled. Within months of the Buddha's death, his followers were resolutely turning his iconoclastic teachings into a respectable Indian religion – with Mahakashyapa leading the effort. Oh, well.

p. 42   An attempt to chronicle the meditator's experience. According to ancient legend, Shakyamuni Buddha had his awakening just as the Morning Star came above the horizon.

p. 44   A poem written for Memorial Day, 2006.

p. 46   ALS changes your body and your relationship to your body. I realized early on that the changes to my body could become a source of fear and aversion or an opportunity to deepen compassion. As a classically trained violist, giving up my hands was particularly difficult.

p. 48   About 50% of ALS patients experience some cognitive decline, with about 20% meeting the criteria for full-blown dementia.

p. 49   No disrespect meant to Dylan Thomas, a great poet – but I've never thought his most famous poem was his best.

p. 54   The 13th century Persian poet Rumi famously wrote "Out beyond ideas of wrongdoing / and rightdoing there is a field. I'll meet you there."

p. 63   An allusion to Moses striking the rock to bring forth water. Exodus 17.

p. 71   This is both the oldest poem in the book, dating from 1988, and also the only poem that has ever made me money. I submitted it to a poetry contest sponsored by a vanity press, and to my great surprise they awarded it first prize and sent me a check for $1000.

p. 73   A poem inspired by reading Robert Bly's book *A Little Book on the Shadow.*

p. 76   Two trees, one in my garden and one in the Garden of Eden. There is nothing in the book of Genesis about Eve eating an apple. The tree in question is called The Tree of the Knowledge of Good and Evil.

p. 78   An imaginative reinterpretation of the classic story of Androcles and the lion.

p. 80   This poem, the following poem, and "Unasked, Unanswered" were all written for a poetic dialogue I had with Wisconsin poet Robin Chapman. The event was organized by *Orion Magazine*, and the goal was for the two of us to exchange poems three times during the month of April, 2014. Robin's wonderful poems inspired me to do some of my best work.

p. 96   The title is a play on words. "Wabi-sabi" is the name of the key aesthetic principle in Japanese art; namely, that nothing is perfect, permanent, or completed.

ABOUT THE AUTHOR

John R. Snyder, poet, musician, computer scientist, and retired Montessori educator, lives in Austin, Texas, with his wife Kathleen. His haiku and renku have been published in literary journals in five countries and translated into several languages. His haiku took first and third prizes at the 2006 World Haiku Festival in the Netherlands. His website is ordinarypersonslife.com.

Made in the USA
Middletown, DE
07 February 2017